YEMAYA

SANTERIA AND THE QUEEN
OF THE SEVEN SEAS

By Baba Raul Canizares

ORIGINAL PUBLICATIONS
Plainview, New York

Yemaya

SANTERIA AND THE QUEEN OF THE SEVEN SEAS

© 2005 by Original Publications

ISBN: 0-942272-86-2

FIRST EDITION

First Printing 2005

Cover Art
by Baba Raul Canizares
Illustrations and Back Cover Art
by Eric K. Lerner

INTRODUCTION

A large group of people gather near the beach in Uruguay, the most European of all Latin American countries, to unveil a large statue depicting a beautiful black woman. In this officially Roman Catholic nation, the government-sanctioned unveiling honors an African goddess, Yemaya, the Yoruba deity of the sea.[1] Although Uruguay is 90% white, a little-known fact about the small nation is that the second largest religion there is Batuque, their version of Orisha worship. The impressive statue was commissioned by Armando Ayala, leader of Batuque in Uruguay and a frequent speaker at Orisha Worship conferences around the world. In attendance is the mayor of Montevideo as well as several important government officials. The reason politicians in Uruguay are warming up to Batuque practitioners is that the religion is growing there at an almost exponential rate, and their votes are just as good as those of Catholics.

It is midnight, February 1st in the banks of Bahia's Rio Vermelho (Red River) in Brazil. Hundreds of thousands gather to send little boats with written petitions, offerings of fruits and flowers, and multi-colored paper flags to Iemanja (Yemaya), the Queen of the Ocean. As the enormous fleet of lighted little vessels sets sail on the river, eventually reaching the sea, the visual effect is stunning. The scene is repeated in greater or lesser scale throughout the Atlantic coast of South America. Without a doubt, the serene, compassionate, beautiful,, and haughty African Queen of the Ocean is the most popular female deity in the New World. In fact, it is only in Cuba where her sister Oshun's popularity surpasses Yemaya's.

In Yorubaland one of the praise names of Yemaya is Olodo, meaning "Owner of Rivers." She is not generally associated with the ocean, but with the large lake that bears her name near Lagos, Nigeria's capital, and with the river Ogun. One can find clues of her future role as the New World's Queen of the Oceans even in Africa. Her enigmatic name in itself suggests an oceanic link, for "Yemaya" is an Hispanicized spelling of the Yoruba "Yemoja," a diminished form of the phrase "yeye omo eja" meaning "mother of the children of fishes." Since most fish are to be found in the ocean, her title implies that most of her children are at sea. So total has Yemaya's identification with the ocean become in the New World that in many Orisha-worshipping communities the actual supremely powerful Lord of the Ocean, Olokun, is considered one of many aspects of Yemaya!

1
Sacred Stories About Yemaya

The following story, now told by many in Nigeria and elsewhere as if it were of ancient origin, was actually invented by a Catholic priest named Noel Baudin in 1884. Colonel A. B. Ellis in his famous work *The Yoruba-Speaking People of the Slave Coast of West Africa (1910)* repeated the story, which was then picked up by countless students of the Yoruba, including the great Brazilian anthropologist Nina Rodrigues.[2] Today, many New World pundits continue to relate the story as if it were a true *pataki,* unaware that it came out of the fertile imagination of a Catholic priest. Before discussing what Father Baudin's motives might have been in fabricating such a myth, let us present the story as it has been repeatedly told, only this time read it knowing it is a total invention having nothing to do with tradition.

From the union of Obatala and Oduduwa, the original pair, came Aganju, the land, and Yemaya, the waters. From the union of Aganju and Yemaya came Orungan, the space that separates heaven from earth. Orungan fell madly in love with his mother, a passion that she tried with all her heart to discourage. One day Orungan couldn't contain himself any longer, so he raped Yemaya. Disgusted and horrified, Yemaya ran as hard as she could, followed by Orungan. Exhausted, Yemaya fell down dead before Orungan could catch up with her. From each of her breasts, two rivers flowed , becoming a lake. From her abdomen, which grew in size until it burst, were born sixteen Orisha: Oko, agriculture; Oshosi, god of the hunt; Shango, god of thunder; Ogun, god of iron; Dada, god of vegetation; Olokun, god of the ocean; Oke, god of the mountains; Shakpana, god of smallpox;

Oshun, goddess of the river Oshun; Oba, goddess of the river Oba; and Oya, goddess of the Niger river

Commentary: This story may reflect Yemaya's great popularity at the time Father Baudin began to spread this very idiosyncratic "pataki." Firstly, we see that the priest was attempting to do in Africa what had already been done successfully in Cuba, to combine the different cults into one religion. Secondly, and perhaps more importantly, naming Orungan as the culprit in the incest story may have been a deliberate attempt on the part of the priest to exonerate Ogun, who according to older stories which traveled with the slaves to Cuba and Brazil was the actual perpetrator. The reasoning for Baudin wanting to do this is clear. Although a Catholic priest, Baudin was apparently an admirer of Yoruba culture and traditions. By the time these events were taking place in the 1840's, Ogun was emerging as an important paragon of truth and justice. In fact, Ogun was becoming one of the few national deities of the Yoruba, and the traditional deity on whose name people took oaths. By choosing a culprit with a similar name—the diminished form of the name "Orungan" is "Ogan," which sounds a lot like "Ogun"—Father Baudin was shifting guilt over the heinous crime from the increasingly influential and important Ogun to the obscure Orungan. So successful was Father Baudin in achieving his goal that in my own lineage in Cuba there are two camps divided over this issue. One side stubbornly sticks to the version having Ogun commit incest not with Yemaya, but with Yemaya's mother, Yemmu. The other side somehow got hold of Baudin's version in the early 1900's, probably through Ellis' writings, and has since mounted an active campaign to clear Ogun's name. I belonged to the latter camp for years, until my training as a researcher in the 1980's forced me to look at the empirical evidence objectively. The facts point to Ogun as the guilty party. For example, both in Cuba and Brazil the story of Ogun's incest with Yemmu is known. Both traditions grew out of the slave trade that brought Yoruba people to these countries beginning in the late

15th century. Since Cuba and Brazil were colonized by competing European powers, Spain and Portugal, slaves brought to one country had virtually no contact with slaves brought to the other.

The fact that in both transplanted Yoruba populations the story of Ogun's incest is known posits the existence of a common source, which would have to be in Yorubaland, the country of origin of both the Lukumi of Cuba and the Nagos of Brazil.

This pataki, a version of which can be found in the odu[3] Ifa Baba Ejiogbe, tells the story of how Orunla married Yemaya Ashaba.[4] It is said that old Yemaya Olokun's daughter Ashaba was so beautiful that all of the Orisha wanted to have her hand in marriage. Compared to most of the Orisha who were seeking Ashaba's hand in marriage, Orunla seemed older, more unassuming, and less attractive. In fact, average-looking Orunla didn't really think he had much of a chance of winning the lovely Ashaba's heart. Like my godfather would say, "Orunla thought he had a better chance of finding a bottle full of wine in the middle of skid row than to get Ashaba to marry him." Orunla, nevertheless, decided to join the coterie of Ashaba's suitors, informing the queen of the ocean that he, too, wanted to be considered for the position of husband to Ashaba. Divining had made Orunla very rich, but compared to the wealth that other suitors had, his wasn't even in the top ten. Before embarking on his quest for the stunning princess' hand Orunla paid his respects to Eshu by offering him a goat. "Open my roads, Little Father, I need you more than ever!" Orunla said. Pleased with the offering, the god who opens paths told Orunla that to gain Ashaba's hand in marriage, he would have to take the following items with him when he went to see her. Two roosters, one hen, a bunch of fish, and two large burlap bags. Although Orunla couldn't imagine why he would be needing such a motley array of things in order to gain Ashaba's heart, he nevertheless did exactly as Eshu had instructed him. It was with his strange hodgepodge of animals and bags that Orunla arrived at Yemaya Olokun's castle.

When Orunla was presented to Ashaba, Eshu turned him inside-out, allowing his inner beauty to be seen by all. Overwhelmed by the beauty of Orunla's heart, which she perceived as extraordinary good looks, Ashaba announced that it would be Orunla she'd marry.

Yemaya Olokun was pleased that Ashaba chose the stable, serious, and wise Orisha, but she had some fears she had to discuss with Orunla.

Yemaya Olokun said: "You've made every male divinity angry! They are so incredibly disconcerted about my daughter choosing you that they have banded together in order to keep you from taking Ashaba away. I know that once you two settle in your realm you will be safe, but your formidable opponents have united their talents to make sure you two don't make it home."

When Orunla took a look outside the castle, he saw that the Orisha had dug a pit on the right side, an abyss on the left side, and a hole as deep as the heavens are high in front. Orunla threw one of the roosters he was carrying into the pit on the right and it closed. He threw the other into the abyss on the left and it closed. He threw the hen in front, which was as deep as the heavens, and it closed. Taking his bride-to-be with him, Orunla escaped his pursuers. The enraged Orisha, however, had prepared a back-up plan in case Orunla managed to escape. In order to reach his domain, Orunla had to cross the great river Ogun. The Orisha had ordered all ferry men on duty not to allow a diviner with a beautiful woman to cross. Orunla used the burlap bags to hide Ashaba inside one bag, filling the other one with fish so it looked as if he was a merchant with his day's purchase of fish for the market. Orunla in disguise as a fisherman made it to the other side.

Once in his domain, Orunla rejoiced and celebrated a grand wedding. The other divinities grudgingly accepted their defeat and attended the feast, presided over by Olofi himself. On a special place of honor sat the best man, Eshu, without whose help Orunla and Ashaba could never have been married. Since that day Orunla's friendship with Eshu became even deeper. That is why all divining boards used by Orunla's spiritual descendants, the babalawo, have an effigy of Eshu

Orunla had to cross the great river Ogun. The Orisha had ordered all ferry men on duty not to allow a diviner with a beautiful woman to cross. Orunla used the burlap bags to hide Ashaba inside one bag, and filled the other with fish.

carved into it, so no babalawo will ever forget to thank Eshu for his unbending devotion to Orunla.

The following pataki, well known in Cuba, relates how Yemaya stole the secret of divining with shells from her husband, Orunla. In Africa it is Oshun who steals the secret, since the present consensus in Yorubaland is that Yemaya was never married to Orunla. Cuban babalawo (priests of Orunla/Ifa), however, steadfastly assert that their version of the story is correct. This is how the story has been told in my lineage for hundreds of years:

Orunla's fame as the greatest diviner kept growing as his wife Yemaya's frustration also grew. You see, Yemaya was born with an insatiable appetite for learning, and she wanted to learn how to divine with cowry shells more than anything. She felt she had a right to divine with shells anyway. After all, wasn't she, as divinity of the sea, the one who collected the shells and brought them to her husband?

But Orunla, an old man set in his ways, wouldn't budge: "No wife of mine is going to be working! You have plenty to do making sure our home is run right."

But Yemaya couldn't give up her dream of being a diviner. Any time she had a chance, she'd sneak a peak when Orunla was divining in order to see what each throw of the shells meant. She also memorized all the chants and incantations that went with each throw.

Eshu, the god of choices, seeing how determined Yemaya was to be a diviner, taught her all the secrets of dilogun (cowry shell divination) behind Orunla's back. The next time Orunla went on an extended trip out of town, Yemaya let it be known that she was available for consultations. So successful was Yemaya that soon she had a larger clientele than her husband. In fact, many of the old man's clients switched over to Yemaya, waiting for Orunla to go out of town so Yemaya would divine for them. Orunla began to notice that, although he was seeing less clients, the home's economic situation seemed to be better!

But Yemaya couldn't give up her dream of being a diviner. Any time she had a chance, she'd sneak a peak when Orunla was divining in order to see what each throw of the shells meant.

"Wife, how is it that although I'm giving you less owo (money) as of lately, we don't seem to be lacking anything. In fact, our standard of living seems to be better?"

"I guess I'm a great administrator, Husband. I just make our money go further."

Orunla had been around too long to be satisfied with his wife's answer. All kinds of disturbing thoughts came to his head. Did his beautiful wife have a lover who supplied her with money? Or worse, was she prostituting herself? The next time Orunla told Yemaya that he was going to be away for several days, he came back, disguised the next day. To his astonishment, many of his clients were lined up in front of his house. Orunla pretended to join the line.

"Excuse me, sir"—Orunla told the elderly gentleman at the end of the line, "but it is my understanding that Orunla is away, so what are we all in line for?"

"We're not here to see Orunla, we're here to see Yemaya. She's even better than he is."

Orunla withheld his rage and waited for his turn. Yemaya was so busy reading for people that she barely looked up to see them, just throwing the dilogun over and over, interpreting them with remarkable intuition and precision. When the disguised Orunla's turn came, Yemaya threw the cowries and all sixteen of them fell face up. This was her husband's own sign—dilogun resembles horoscopes in this manner, people being associated with the personality types expressed in the odu, configurations, that come up for them. Irete, sixteen shells up, comes up only rarely. Immediately, Yemaya realized she was in front of her enraged husband. Fearing her husband's violent temper (Orunla rarely lost his temper, but when he did he was extremely violent), Yemaya ran as fast as she could, with Orunla in hot pursuit after her. Yemaya first went to Obatala seeking refuge, but the Great Father refused to interfere with his daughter's marital problem. She then asked her brother Aganju to hide her, but he also refused. Finally, she went by the beach, where a group of adodi (gay males) were merrily frolicking in the waters. Knowing how Orunla disliked associating with homosexuals, Yemaya asked the young men to hide her. She knew that Orunla wouldn't even get near people he strongly disapproved of. "Sure thing, girlfriend, just come on over and join the party," a tall, handsome youth told her. When Orunla arrived at the scene, he stayed a respectable distance away and demanded that his wife be turned over.

The group of men, who were enjoying a day at the beach and had imbibed a good quantity of alcohol, which made them feel tipsy and in a playful mood, told Orunla: "Why don't you come over and get her, big boy."

"Yeah, baby,"another one chimed in. "And give us a little kiss while you're at it!"

Disgusted, Orunla went back home, where he cooled off, regaining his usual composure. In the meantime, Yemaya thanked each of her protectors and swore from then on to be a champion of gay men. "I'll be your Orisha!" Yemaya tearfully said. This is why to this day gay men have a special love for Yemaya.

When Yemaya eventually went back home, Orunla said he'd forgive her for her transgression. In fact, Orunla was inwardly glad that it was by divining that Yemaya was making money, and not in other ways he had contemplated. But she would have to give up her practice.

"There can only be one diviner under my roof, me."

With great pain, because she truly cared for Orunla, Yemaya said: "A sad and frustrated wife you do not deserve, and if I can't realize my dream of being a diviner, I therefore must leave my husband in order to realize myself"

So upset was Orunla that Yemaya had learned to use the cowry shell oracle that he swore from that day onward never to use cowry shells again. Orunla had received from Olodumare (God Almighty) the gift of drumming and dancing better than anyone on earth, a gift the studious Orisha didn't particularly appreciate. Shango, in the meantime, had been giving a divining chain called Okpele and a set of divining nuts called ikin which were incredibly accurate. Knowing how much Shango enjoyed drumming and dancing, Orunla offered to make a trade with the Orisha of thunder, would he give up his divining tools in exchange for Orunla's musical gifts? Shango was ecstatic with the exchange, so with God's permission, the two Orisha exchanged gifts. This is why to this day babalawo, Orunla's spiritual descendants, will not use cowry shells for divination, but the okpele and the ikin.

In the meantime, Yemaya taught her little sisters Oshun and Oya how to divine using the shells. The business-minded Oya proposed that they become partners forming a joint practice. Oshun proposed that they also bring in Eshu-Laroye, Lord of Communications, to handle the advertising. They all agreed to divide each day's take equally in four parts. Soon the firm of Yemaya, Oshun, Oya, and Laroye, cowry shell divination experts, flourished. They acquired a comfortable place by the beach, where Laroye would send them client after client. He would stand in a bustling intersection telling everyone about the sisters. In the beginning all was well, the considerable bounty that was collected each day would be fairly divided among the four partners. Soon, however, the three sisters began to have doubts about Laroye, thinking they were paying him too much. At first they began to cut his part a little here and there, until they finally stopped giving him anything.

At that point, Laroye stood by the road that led to the beach house, turning all clients away. "Yemaya, Oshun, and Oya do not live here anymore," Eshu Laroye would say.

After a few days, the sisters called Laroye up to speak with him.

"Where are the clients?" Oya wanted to know.

"We are starving here!" said Oshun.

"I guess the clients went the same way my part of the profits went," Laroye answered. "I haven't seen any for days!"

Soon the firm of Yemaya, Oshun, Oya, and Laroye, cowry shell divination experts, flourished.

Yemaya immediately recognized the wrong they had committed and asked Laroye for forgiveness.

"Furthermore," the regal beauty stated, "Eshu Laroye's profit will be the first separated, his food will be the first served, his portion of money the first taken aside for him." The sisters did this and their practice again flourished.

Commentary: There is enough material in this pataki to engage a serious student a lifetime. Although at least a couple of hundred years old, the themes the pataki touches on couldn't be more current.

These include: male chauvinism; the need for women to redefine their role in society; housewife versus career woman; and the need for businesses to act in an ethical manner. Interestingly, this pataki is one of at least ten that addresses the issue of homosexuality. What I find fascinating is that in this particular religion, which has roots as ancient as those of any other living faith, homosexuals are always portrayed either in a neutral light or, as is the case in this story, in a positive light. This may be one of the reasons why gays seem to be over-represented in Orisha Worship, because it is perhaps the only one of the ancient traditions that neither ignores them nor judges them, where they are in fact portrayed as being a natural part of everyday life. The one taboo gays have concerns the priesthood of Orunla, who forbade his followers to ordain gay men or women.[6] Priests of Orunla, however, do not consider themselves a part of Santeria, but a closely allied faith called Ifa. In Santeria proper, women and gays can occupy any position.

Proving that Catholic priests are not the only ones who can come up with bizarre pseudo-pataki involving Yemaya, we have the Cuban invention of how the Queen of the Ocean granted Oshun's wish to change appearance from dark-skinned African with "nappy" hair to honey-colored mulata with long, wavy hair. Risible in its absurdity, the story has taken such hold in Cuba that hardly anyone disputes its veracity. When I tell this story in public I sometimes call it "Oshun does a Michael Jackson four hundred years before Michael Jackson." The story goes something like this:

During the shameful days of the slave trade, Oshun saw thousands upon thousands of her devotees being taken away to faraway lands. Frustrated, the Orisha of rivers was somehow unable to keep this horrible deed from occurring. As she often did when troubled, Oshun sought solace in the maternal arms of her big sister, Queen Yemaya, who told her that there were some mysteries not even the Orisha could decipher.

"Yemaya, you whose oceans touch every land, where are all our children being taken to?"

"They are being taken to many places. See those ships there in the harbor?" The stately queen pointed to two large vessels. "They are going to end up in Cuba. In fact, many of our people will end up in Cuba."

Becoming pensive for a moment, Oshun asked Yemaya, "What is Cuba like?"

"It is very much like here, lush vegetation, tranquil rivers, beautiful beaches, clear blue skies."

"What about the people, Dear Sister, are they like us?"

"No, they are not all black like us. Some are black, some are white, some are red, some are brown, and a few are yellow."

Without thinking twice, Oshun said: "I want to go with them! I want to be there to help my children in this their hour of need! But before I go, Yemaya, you who knows so many secrets of the ocean depths, make my hair straighter and my complexion lighter so that all Cubans can see a little of themselves in me!"

With a majestic sweep of her hand Yemaya changed Oshun's hair from extremely curly to long and wavy, and her complexion from dark ebony to golden honey. Shortly after her arrival in Cuba, everyone fell in love with Oshun, the island being dedicated to Oshun by all the elders. All Cubans, no matter what the color of their skins, worship their beloved *bella mulata* together.

Commentary: This transparently obvious fabrication was concocted to explain why Oshun is depicted as a woman of mixed ancestry. On a deeper level, however, this story demonstrates the overwhelming popularity of Oshun in Cuba.

The following pataki talks about how death came to the world. In the beginning, the old ones came down to earth, leaving Iku behind to keep Olodumare company. The old ones had children, but no one died. So the children were forever destined to be subservient to the old ones. Yemaya, one of the young ones, thought this was an unfair state of affairs.

She told her fellow young ones "Not only among our kind, but the humans, also, are suffering the same fate. The first humans created hold all the positions of power, and since they are immortal, they will never give their descendants the opportunity to hold positions of leadership."

Yemaya went to heaven and asked Olodumare to send Iku down to start killing the old ones. She said, "That way everyone will have the opportunity to grow, then die, letting someone young grow, and then die." And so it was that Iku came down to earth and from that day on nobody rules forever, and progress entered the world.

2
ATTRIBUTES

Necklace: Yemaya's "generic" all-purpose necklace is usually made up of seven dark blue beads followed by seven clear beads, continuing the pattern until desired length is achieved. Different paths, however, have different patterns. Yemaya Asesu, for example, takes turquoise-colored beads instead of dark blue, and opaque white beads instead of clear.

Shrine (igbodu) How initiates honor Yemaya: Yemaya's secrets are usually kept in a blue and white soup tureen. These include seven black river stones, about twenty-one cowry shells, and the herramientas (tools) of Yemaya, which are made of silver, lead, or nickel. These are: a sun (oru), a full moon (oshu), an anchor (dakoduro), lifesaver (yika), boat (oko), seven oars (alami), seven bracelets (bopa), a skeleton key (chileku), and a star (irawo). An iruke (fly whisk) decorated with blue and white beads adorns the shrine, as well as a small bell (agogo), and a fan made of mother of pearl and gold-colored material (abebe).

Shrine (olujo alejo) How non-initiates may begin to honor Yemaya: An altar containing sand, dried starfish, small mermaid figurines, shells, and anything to do with the ocean can be set up as a focus of devotion to Yemaya. The traditional altar non-initiates maintained in Cuba was fashioned out of a glass bowl, water to which indigo or another bluing agent was added, seven pennies, some shells, and a rubber ducky! A small figurine of the Virgin of Regla was usually placed in the middle of the bowl, on top of a coral stone or something along that fashion.

Offerings (adimu): Yemaya's favorite offering is a whole watermelon in which a small square opening has been made, some of the pulp taken out, molasses put in, and the piece that had been taken out replaced as a lid, covering the molasses. The entire watermelon is then offered to the sea.

Blood offerings (ebo): Sheep, roosters, guinea fowl, tortoises, ducks, parrots, geese, quails, and roaches (which she calls her "cracklings"). Yemaya Asesu takes pig sacrifices. Yemaya Ocute hates ducks.

Characteristics of Yemaya (and of her children): Yemaya's feast day in Cuba is celebrated September 7th or, in some lineages, September 12th. Her color is blue, her number 7. Yemaya is syncretized in Cuba with Our Lady of Regla. Although I've read non-Cuban writers translating this as "Our Lady of Rules," going as far as to say that the reason this Catholic image was chosen by Santeros to represent the Orisha is because Yemaya loves rules and order. This is nonsense.

Baba Adekun explains the origin of our Lady of Regla and her syncretism with Yemaya in Original Publications *The Magick and Powers of Saints:*

> The original statue of this avocation of the Virgin was sculpted in Africa according to legend in the Fourth Century CE! When the Monastery that housed the statue was attacked, the monks fled with the statue to Spain. Around 1330, an apparition of the Virgin appeared to an Augustine monk in Leon, Spain. Reportedly she told him where the statue had been buried, indicating its position with a ball of fire, and that a Cathedral must be erected there. The monk allegedly dug up the statue. The statue was then housed in the Church. Around 1735, the people of Poona Spain chose Our Lady of the Rules as their patroness, and miracles began to be attributed to her.

It is important to note that she has always been depicted as a black woman, and the original statue resembles an Afrikan deity from Benin or Yorubaland... When her icons traveled to Cuba, she became identified with the great orisha Yemaya. There is an amusing story about a priest in Cuba whose Church enjoyed sudden popularity when a statue of La Regla was installed. It is said that the priest initially attributed the sudden influx of practitioners to his preaching. Imagine his shock when he discovered that Yoruba religious practitioners had placed Afrikan textiles associated with Yemaya under the Madonna's Catholic robes. The congregation had come to venerate Yemaya!

Strong-willed, independent women are often daughters of Yemaya. Children of Yemaya tend to be nurturing and selfless, yet also haughty and of regal bearing. They hold grudges. Children of Yemaya love luxury and can be overly observant of hierarchical structures.

In my 1992 work *Walking with the Night, the Afro-Cuban World of Santeria* (Rochester, VT: Inner Traditions International), since re-named *Cuban Santeria: Walking with the Night* (1999), I dedicated a whole chapter to the proposition that Santeria is fast becoming a world religion, a reality joyfully celebrated by many Santeros beaten down by many years of mistreatment at the hands of so-called "mainstream religions," but not by me! Every time pop culture gets its hands on an indigenous practice, it turns it into a flaccid hybrid devoid of power and full of empty decorative fluff. This is why it was with some trepidation that I told the affluent-looking society matron getting a reading from me that the shells indicated Yemaya wanted her to become a Santera. As it turned out, there was more to Margaret than met the eye. Yes, she was a sophisticated Manhattanite, but she had also led an unconventional and incredibly fascinating life. By the time she came for a reading in 1995 she and her husband had crossed the Atlantic alone in their small craft (she was the inspiration for the character played by Kathleen Turner in the movie Romancing the Stone), had spent time with the Hindu man-god Satya Sai Baba, had helped write the famous book *The "G" Spot*, had penned several Nancy Drew mysteries and had been one of guru Hilda Charlton's original students. Daughter of one of the most powerful attorneys in America, Margaret was not what one would consider a natural follower of Santeria. In fact, before her reading, she had never heard of Santeria or Yemaya. In her initial reading, I divined that Yemaya was Margaret's mother and that she was destined to become a priestess of the Sea Goddess. Within three months Margaret made Santo, since then she has become a powerful priestess who has helped hundreds through her practice. Identifying with the goddess has become Margaret's defining characteristic. Her case showed me that Orisha worship is truly universal, and that by limiting its scope I was actually perpetrating the stereotypes I thought I was fighting. Margaret has demonstrated that there is no "typical" person who can benefit from Orisha worship, just as there is no typical Catholic or typical Protestant.

Yemaya protects people from drowning or from suffering due to torrential rains or floods. She is also the Orisha that protects the lower torso and the buttocks against illnesses and mishaps. Yemaya is also identified with female breasts.

Yemaya's identification with motherhood comes from her identification with the uppermost layers of the sea, where all life began. As Gary Edwards and John Mason have written, "The ocean is . . . the most fruitful of surroundings, and acts as a womb for the generation of life."[7]

Herbs and plants: Marjoram, watermelon (her favorite), cilantro, watercress, lettuce, aloe vera, indigo, fern, bell pepper, lotus, violet, and vervain.

ROADS OF YEMAYA:

Alara: Yemaya as a refined beauty.

Ashaba, Ayaba: "A wise and helpful path, Ashaba wears a silver anklet. She has a hard look—she'll stare you down—and haughty air. In this avatar she was married to Orunla, from whom she stole the secret of how to divine with cowry shells. She works as God's secretary."[8]

Asesu: Said to be a messenger of Olofi—God himself, she is represented by turbulent waters. She is allied to the dead and is known as being meticulous and slow.

Awoyo: "The oldest Yemaya, the one who wears the most luxurious clothes, the one who puts on seven skirts in order to fight and defend her children . . . When she goes out on the town, Awoyo wears Olokun's accessories and Oshumare, the rainbow, for a crown."[9]

Akuara: "The Yemaya of two waters, where the river converges with the ocean, there she lives, in fresh water, along with her sister Oshun. She likes to dance and have fun, she is not strict at all. She will not cause harm. She heals the sick, prepares remedies, and helps women who suffer stillbirths." [10]

Konla: The foam of the sea.

Gunle: The seashore personified.

Mayele, Mayelewo: "Lives in the forest, in a well, or a spring. She is Oshun Ibu Kole's sister, both are sorceresses. Mayelewo is close to Ogun."[11]

Ogunte, Okute: "Her color is light blue. She is found in the coral reefs. She is Olokun's handmaiden. She is found both in fresh and salty waters. In this avatar, Yemaya is married to the god of Iron, Ogun. She receives offerings along with Ogun, and can be "fed" either at sea or in the bush. A warrior manifestation, this Yemaya is a tireless worker. She wears Ogun's tools on a belt. She has the bearing of an intimidating amazon, the mouse is her animal. She dislikes dogs. Yemaya Okute has a vile temper, is very austere, and holds grudges... in this road Yemaya doesn't like to eat duck, preferring lamb. She wears coral and mother-of-pearl adornments."[12]

Olodo: The owner of all rivers.

Olokun: The sea. Although actually a separate Orisha, many houses in Cuba consider Olokun a path of Yemaya.

Owoyo: The crescent moon.

Yemaya Ye Ile Lodo: In this path offerings of lamb must be deposited at sea, river, or in the home.

Ayaba Ti Gbe Ibu Omi: Mother of Shango de Ima, an avatar of Shango.

Tinibo: The rough seas personified.

Agana: An Egbado path

Awo Sama: Queen of rain clouds

Yalodde: Great Queen

Ibu Ina: Thermal waters, volcanic waters.

Ibu Koto, Okoto: Personified by reddish stones near the coast.

In Arara religion Yemaya is called Afrekete. In Palo she is known as Mama Kalunga, Madre de Agua, and Balaunde.

Yemaya in Brazil: More people practice Orisha worship in Brazil than in any other country, including Nigeria, yet one doesn't hear much about their practices outside the country. This is due to the extreme hermeticism carried out by priesthood holders there, and because of their unwillingness to allow the religion to be exported. As many priests and priestesses of Brazilian Orixa come to live in the United States, however, an inevitable shift will occur towards more openness, and their version of the religion will become more accessible to others, as Cuban Santeria has.

In Brazilian Candomble, their equivalent of Cuban Santeria, Yemaya is called Iemanja. She is also known as Dona Janaina. Her color is light blue. Her necklace is made up entirely of clear beads. In Brazil Yemaya accepts offerings of female goats, hens, and

The most popular image of Iemanja in Brazil is of a voluptuous young
light-skinned woman with very long black hair emerging from the sea.

ducks. Her day of the week is Saturday, her feast days December 8th and February 2nd. She is syncretized with the Immaculate Conception. As in Cuba Oshun became a light-skinned, long-haired woman, the most popular image of Iemanja in Brazil is of a voluptuous young light-skinned woman with very long black hair emerging from the sea. She is also often depicted as a mermaid. Iemanja rivals Xango as the most popular Orixa in Brazil.

Initiation names: At a recent initiation ceremony, where an Orisha name is selected for the neophyte through the use of the oracle, I was appalled to see that after about seven tries, each time the oracle saying "no" to the name the oriate proposed, the oriate looked blankly around, for he had run out of names! Luckily, those of us who were present and knew other proper names to offer saved the situation. Respected elder Andres Hing (Chango Yemi) published the following list of allowed names for Yemaya in 1971.[13]

Omi Yale;Omi Tola; Omi Diero; Omi Kunle; Ofofunloro; Oshabi;Omi Tonade; Omi Tode; Omi Saya; Omi Lari; Omi Wale Iyawere; Omi Leti; Omi Tinibu; Fadiese; Asinabi; Omi Tawade; Oloyomi Misande; Omi Toke; Omi Yomi; Omi Tirle; Omi Keye; Omi Aladora; Omi Sainde; Omi Sayade; Oreku; Omi Tomi; Omi Simi; Omi Dina; Odomi;Olomidara; Omi Lana.

3
YEMAYA AND SANTERIA'S "CELESTIAL COURT"

In Africa, Orisha worshippers generally belong to a society ("egbe") dedicated to the worship of a single Orisha. Thus, worshippers of Obatala would belong to Egbe Obatala, those who worship Yemaya would belong to Egbe Yemaya and so forth. These societies were in fact denominations, fully self-sufficient and not necessarily having anything to do with initiations into Orishas other than their own. The three elements of Orisha worship that transcended the boundaries of egbe were Elegbara worship, ancestor veneration ("egungun") and Ifa divination. Elegbara was worshipped across the board because, as the Orisha who opens and closes doors, both literal and metaphysical, he could keep anyone from achieving anything. The ancestors, of course, form the backbone of most indigenous spiritualities, for it is in great part deified ancestors who receive the greatest amount of worship in many of these primal societies. Ifa priests have attained great fame and respect as codifiers, recorders, and teachers of Orisha worship. Although strictly speaking they are one more egbe among many, in reality they are the scholars of Orisha worship and have attained the status of high priests.

During the shameful days of the slave trade, members of all egbes were criminally brought to the Americas. Due to the horrible conditions endured by these brave men, women, and children, they found their lives interrupted in a fashion so lacking in humanity it is hard for us today to imagine our ancestors being subjected to such ignominy just a few generations ago. Members of different egbes would be grouped together in different plantations. Lacking the infrastructures they had enjoyed in their homeland, egbes that in Africa would have nothing to do with each other became associated by necessity. A member of Egbe Oshun, for example, would teach a member of Egbe Obatala about his religion, while the member of Obatala's egbe would reciprocate. In this fashion, each worshipper made sure his or her Orisha would not fall into oblivion. Eventually, a synthesis began to occur where the egbes began to become fused into a single religion, Lukumi, also called "Regla de Ocha" and Santeria.

Where the ashe of a single Orisha would be revealed to an initiate in Africa, a standard five Orisha were offered automatically in a Santeria initiation, though only one of these would be installed in a person's head. The five standard Orishas were Elegbara (Eleggua), Obatala, Shango, Yemaya, and Oshun.

Our elders referred to the Lukumi pantheon as *"la corte celestial,"* The Celestial Court, presided by the divine emperor Obatala Obaigbo and his empress Obatala Yemmu. Under Obatala, certain Orisha were given honor as kings and queens. Shango is the most obvious embodiment of the Yoruba ideal of the perfect king. Aganju and Ogun also have very distinct paths where they are addressed as kings. Babalu Aye is thought to have had to leave his native land, going to the land of Arara (Dahomey) where he was proclaimed king. Olokun is the powerful ruler of the ocean depths. Of the female Orisha, only two are thought to be queens in their own rights, Oya and Yemaya. The rest are thought of as either consorts or daughters of monarchs.

The equivalent of a royal scepter among the Yoruba is the iruke, a fly whisk made out of the tail of a horse. According to the elders, only Oya and Yemaya among female Orisha have a right to use an iruke. Oya was the queen of Nupe before she joined any man. She later joined her kingdom with that of Shango, but she never gave up the throne, ruling alongside her husband. Yemaya's kingdom is the sea, specifically the upper regions of the ocean, where sunlight makes it possible for a variety of life forms to develop. In many ways, Yemaya is depicted in Cuban Santeria as an example of how a queen should act. She is majestic yet not snobbish, exquisitely attired yet not gaudy, strong yet not strident. And she lovingly takes maternal care of all the children her sometimes frivolous sisters neglect. Her association with her sister Oshun is unwavering. The pataki relating her many tender ministrations to Oshun whenever she has had need of Yemaya's wise counsel are among the most touching in Santeria.

Along with Obatala, Shango, Oshun, and Oya, Yemaya is one of the most commonly "seated" Orisha in Cuban Santeria. Although no formal surveys have been conducted to determine what percentage of all Santeros are priests and priestesses of Yemaya, I wouldn't be surprised if it were twenty-five percent or more.

Yemaya's dignified demeanor and motherly warmth gives comfort and solace to all Santeria practitioners. Her place as a queen in her own right makes her one of the most important members of Santeria's Celestial Court.

4
ORIKI YEMAYA
ORIN YEMAYA
(PRAYERS AND SONGS
TO YEMAYA)

Those who have been initiated as priests and priestesses in Santeria can increase the power of cleansings and works they do with Yemaya by reciting praise verses called "oriki" and by singing praise songs called "Orin" (also called "suyere") to the Orisha. Following are some oriki and Orin in Lukumi that have been in use in Cuba for hundreds of years. Speakers of standard Yoruba should be able in most cases to recognize the meaning of the Lukumi words.

Oriki

O mio Yemaya!

Mother of the Children of Fishes

Mother of the Waters of the Ocean

Mother of the Waters of the Rain

Mother of the Waters of the Rivers

Mother of the Waters of the Streams

That flow under the Earth

Your beautiful breasts hang full of nourishing milk

Your belly opens and gods are born

O mio Yemaya!

Mother of the Children of Fishes
Mother of the children of other mothers
Mother of the World
Let me sit with my loved ones
In the hole left by your buttocks in the sand

Oriki

Da fun Walami
Ti s'ajele Oko
Ma ma j'Oko o da
Walami
Ma ma si j'Oko da
Walami

Look for the paddle,
Servant of boat
Do not let the boat capsize
paddle
Do not let the boat capsize

Oriki (Uruguay)

Soy hija del mar,
hija de las olas,

Hija de la espuma,
Oh mi madre, Yemaya,
Reina del salobre mar,
Oh mi madre, Yemaya,
Baja y ven donde mi.

I am the daughter of the sea,
Daughter of the waves,
Daughter of the ocean foam.
Oh my mother, Yemaya,
Queen of the salt sea,
Oh my mother, Yemaya,
Come down and counsel me.

Orin

Yemaya Asesu Asesu Yemaya
Yemaya Asesu Asesu Yemaya
Yemaya Olodo
Olodo Yemaya
Yemaya Olodo
Olodo Yemaya
Yemaya of the gushing spring
Of the gushing spring, Yemaya
Yemaya of the gushing spring

Of the gushing spring, Yemaya
Yemaya Owner of Rivers
Owner of rivers, Yemaya
Yemaya Owner of Rivers
Owner of rivers, Yemaya.

Orin

Kai! Kai! Kai! Yemaya Olodo,
Kai! Kai! Kai! Iya mi Olodo.

Kai! Kai! Kai! Yemaya Olodo,
Kai! Kai! Kai! Iya mi Olodo.

Hear ye! Hear ye! Hear ye! Yemaya owns all rivers.
Hear ye! Hear ye! Hear ye! My Mother owns all rivers!

Hear ye! Hear ye! Hear ye! Yemaya owns all rivers.
Hear ye! Hear ye! Hear ye! My Mother owns all rivers!

Orin

Orisha re mi olowo,
omolowo a ki Yemaya

Orisha re mi olowo,

omolowo a ki Yemaya

The goddess gives me blessings, I'm rich. I am a child of wealth, I salute Yemaya.

The goddess gives me blessings, I'm rich. I am a child of wealth, I salute Yemaya.

Orin (Brazil)

Ba uba-a

Ba uba-a

A woyo

Sarele

Yewashe

Awade

Iyade lode

Ba uba

Onibo to ile

Aya onibo to ile

Onibo iwya

Iya bibo ile

If we do not meet her

If we do not meet her

Though we look for her long
We shall hasten to humble ourselves
Before our mother the lawgiver
We have arrived
Our mother is outside
Should we not meet her?
The wife of one who protects the house
One who nourishes, the queen
The mother who nourishes the household

5
DESPOJOS/CLEANSINGS AND SPELLS WITH YEMAYA

Yemaya is a refined queen. She adores fine foods, especially the fruits of the sea, such as shrimps, fish, and lobsters. Preparing a fine meal for Yemaya, then passing the meal (on a plate) over your body before offering it to the sea is an excellent cleansing to rid yourself of bad vibrations and bring the blessing of money to your household.

YEMAYA'S FAVORITE RECIPES

Yemaya's favorite dish is called Ochinchin de Yemaya. This is how we prepare it in my house. Take a pound of cleaned, de-veined shrimp, four ounces of bottled capers (similar to olives), six hard-boiled eggs (cut in halves), about six ounces of cooked collard greens, a small onion (diced), and one medium-sized red tomato (diced) in one quart of boiling water. Add a teaspoon of oil, a teaspoon of salt, the shrimp, empty the bottle of capers, liquid and all, into the boiling water. Add the greens, the onion, and the tomato. Simmer for a half hour. Garnish with fresh watercress.

It is said that Yemaya will grant you any wish if you give her a watermelon that has been saturated with plenty of molasses. The way to do this is to cut a square on the watermelon, saving it to use as a lid later. Scoop out enough red pulp to allow a bottle of molasses to be emptied into the hole. As the molasses slowly pours out of the bottle, make your petitions. Replace the "lid," and take the melon to the ocean, leaving seven pennies in the water. Within twenty-one days your (reasonable) petitions will be granted. Wise and ancient advice is: be careful what you ask for, because you might just get it!

CLEANSINGS WITH YEMAYA

The most powerful cleansing you can do with Yemaya is to go to the beach, enter the water sideways, not frontally or backwards, submerge yourself totally one, three, or seven times, asking Yemaya to cleanse you. Always leave a monetary offering of seven pennies.

A variation of the above cleansing is to rip off your old clothes in the ocean, letting the tide take the old clothes away. Then wear new clothes as you leave the beach, signifying that you want Yemaya to help you achieve some kind of renewal in your life.

Bathing with watercress brings blessings of health, while bathing with parsley brings Yemaya's blessings of money.

Keeping, near the front door, a glass bowl filled with blue water, to which seven pennies, some seashells, a piece of coral, and a rubber ducky has been added, will bring good luck to the household.

LOVE SPELLS

Assemble a watermelon, oil of cloves, olive oil, almond oil, seven straight pins, molasses, red mercury, and a piece of brown paper on which is written the names of the two people who are to be made to fall in love. Annoint the watermelon with the oils and molasses. Then secure the petition to the melon with the seven pins. Place the melon in the bag. Sprinkle the mercury powder over the melon before closing the bag. After seven days throw the bag and contents into the ocean.

Another love spell goes like this: write name of person you want to influence, pierce a small watermelon with seven straight pins.

Take a smooth-surfaced river stone, red mercury, and rock candy and place these ingredients, along with the melon, on a plate. After seven days, offer this to the ocean. It will turn an indifferent man or woman into an attentive lover.

An old priestess of Yemaya once told me that the most powerful spell to make a woman fall in love with a man is to get some shit from a bitch in heat (the canine kind), let it dry, ground to a powder, and just blow that powder on the object of your affection. No woman can resist this spell!

In her wonderful tome *Yemaya y Ochun*, the great Cuban ethnographer Lydia Cabrera gave the recipe for what she calls the "Mother Formula" or most potent attraction essence ever designed:

In a gallon jug, gather together the following ingredients (preferably on a Good Saturday of Easter week): cinnamon extract, anise extract, teaspoon of lemon juice, apple blossom extract, rosemary, benzoin, holy water, ground yam, sandalwood, a slug [a snail can be substituted], three different kinds of mercury [16], some moonshine liquor, some rum, petals from the following four flowers: forget-me-nots, pansies, roses, and lillies. Rue, mimosa, yamao, parami, amansa guapo, and duermete puta.[17] Add High John the Conqueror root and three drops of your urine to the mix, plus the urine of a bitch in heat, say the prayer of Anima Sola three times, and leave the gallon by Eleggua's altar for three days. This perfume is to be used on the hands, face, and handkerchief of person who will now be irresistible[18]

Another one of Cabrera's informants, Nina, the self-described "Santera to fine white ladies" offered the following recipe for an attraction powder: Expensive after-shower body powder mixed with apple blossom extract and ground basil. [19] Although much less complicated when compared to the "Mother Formula," Nina swore by her powder.

MONEY SPELLS

The following work is said to be unfailing to bring wealth through Yemaya's auspices. Go to the beach, taking with you a coconut, an indigo block or ball (sold at all botanicas) some olive oil, a floating wick, and a bough of basil. Break coconut in two, empty most of its juice. Add all ingredients, light wick and say the following incantation over the lamp you've just made: "Awa rere Ogun omodi ofomo oyu Iya Abila." Leave lamp on the shore of the beach, go back home and wear nothing but blue during the next seven days. Yemaya will reward you with great wealth.

A Yemaya bath guaranteed to bring the blessing of money consists of filling your tub with cold water (as cold as you can stand it), then adding seven bunches of parsley and five of watercress to the water, as well as a cup of whole milk and seven pennies. Light a blue candle and a green candle while bathing. Leave all remains of the bath (inside a garbage bag) at night as close to the door of a bank as possible.

To gain Yemaya's favor, do as old Santeras do in Matanzas province, Cuba, where very serious practitioners of Orisha worship have resided for a very long time. Cook up a great meal with white steamed rice, black bean soup, and fried pork cooked with onion rings, garlic, salt, cumin, and lime juice. Offer it sizzling hot to Yemaya, along with a slice of watermelon. She'll give you whatever you want!

YEMAYA'S RECIPE FOR RASPBERRY LEAF TEA

Gather fresh raspberry leaves (wild or cultivated) from an organic source. Tie in bunches with twine and hang upside down in a warm, dark, well-ventilated area until dry (about two weeks). Strip the leaves from the branches and crumble the leaves. Brew leaves for tea. Raspberry leaves strengthen the lining of the uterus and invigorate all female reproductive organs.

YEMAYA'S FERTILITY BATH

Watermelon
Sea water
Lotus flower
Kelp
Florida Water
Seven Pennies
Blue candle

Cut the petals of the flower into small pieces and place in a large bowl. Pour sea water over petals, then add a splash of Florida water. Cut a small hole in the watermelon, put pennies inside and place the entire watermelon next to the bowl with the cut-up flower and sea water. Light the candle in honor of Yemaya and allow all to stand for 3 days. On the 3rd day, scoop the pennies and some flesh out of the watermelon. Add this to the bowl, and then add everything from the bowl to your bath water. Remain in it for twenty-five minutes, imagining your belly filled with a healthy baby.

YEMAYA FERTILITY OIL
(For women)

7 drops Watermelon
3 drops Balsam
1 drop Aster

Use freely as you would any perfumed oil.

YEMAYA' S FERTILITY OIL LAMP

One watermelon
2 cups Molasses
3 cups Olive Oil
1 cup Dry rice & beans(mixed together)
1 tablespoon confectioner's sugar
1 tablespoon each shredded coconut
1 ball of anil (indigo or bluing)
1 cup river sand
1 cup sea water
1 cup fresh basil leaves
7 pennies
1 tea light

Cut watermelon into two parts lengthwise and scoop most of the
insides out of one. Write your name 7 times on a piece of brown
paper bag and place in the bottom of one half the watermelon.
On top of the paper place the 7 pennies and 7 of the watermelons
seeds. Next, place the sugar, coconut, basil & rice and beans inside
the melon. When this is done, pour water in, then the molasses
and the oil. Mix the anil with the oil. Then float the tea light on
the prepared oil. Light the candle and allow it to burn for 7 days,
replacing wick as needed. On the eighth day, leave the oil lamp
(the watermelon and its contents) on the beach near the ocean.

APHRODISIAC DRINK
DEDICATED TO YEMAYA

2 cups white rum
1 cup gin
1/2 cup syrup of raspberries
1 cup lemon juice
Ice cubes

Shake it and serve to your partner (you may drink some if needed).

TO KNOW IF YOU'LL HAVE A GOOD YEAR
(BRAZIL)

On New Year's Eve, at midnight, go to a beach and light a candle in Yemaya's name. Then, set a little boat covered with flowers adrift on the waves. If the boat is taken out to the sea by Yemaya, it will be a good year for you. If the boat is refused and comes back onto the sand, it will be a bad year.

Endnotes

1. The Yoruba people once formed a powerful empire on the West coast of Africa. Today most of them occupy the Southwestern portion of the modern nation of Nigeria.

2. Nina Rodrigues. Os *Africanos no Brasil* (Rio de Janeiro: Editorial Nacional, 1945) p. 353.

3. An "odu" is one of 256 chapters of the Ifa corpus, the sacred scriptures—formerly orally transmitted—of Ifa religion.

4. See Conrad E. Mauge, Ph.D. *Odu Ifa: Book One: Sacred Scriptures of Ifa: Eji Ogbe* (Mount Vernon, NY: House if Providence) p. 17.

5. I realize that the way this tale is presented—associating gay males with a certain kind of frivolity—may seem offensive to some, but I've decided to put the story down exactly as I heard it since, when viewed in context, it exhibits remarkable tolerance and valor.

6. This prohibition seems to be in effect only in the Cuban lineages. There are many ordained women priests of Ifa in Africa and, according to Wande Abimbola, spokesman for babalawo around the world, they have a "don't ask, don't tell" policy about gays over there. (See Dr. Abimbola's book *Ifa Will Mend Our Broken World* (Roxbury, MA: Aim Books, 1997).

7. Gary Edwards and John Mason. *Black Gods: Orisha Studies in the New World* (Brooklyn, NY: Y.T.A., 1985) p.86.

8. Natalia Bolivar Arostegui, *Los Orishas en Cuba* (Havana: Ediciones Union, 1990) p. 95.

9. ibid.

10. ibid., p.96.

11. ibid.

12. ibid.

13. Andres Hing. *Oddun de Ifa al Caracol"* Self-Published, 1971.

14. Collected by Paco Cuevas in Benin state, Nigeria.

15. Harold Courlander. *Tales of Yoruba Gods and Heroes* (Plainview, NY: Original Publications, 1973) p.229.

16. Because of the dangers associated with use of mercury, either use extremely little or dispense with this ingredients.

17. I don't know the English names of these, but most well-stocked botanical will carry them.

18. Lydia Cabrera, *Yemaya y Ochun* (Madrid: C.R., 1974) p.313.

19. ibid.

ITEM #216
$9.95

HELPING YOURSELF WITH SELECTED PRAYERS VOLUME 2
Now With 170 Prayers!

The prayers from Volume 2 come from diverse sources. Most originated in Roman Catholicism and can still be found in one form or another on the reverse of little pocket pictures of saints, or in collections of popular prayers. Another source for these prayers is the French Spiritist movement begun in the 1800's by Allan Kardec, which has become a force in Latin America under the name Espiritismo. The third source, representing perhaps the most mystical, magical, and practical aspects of these prayers, is found among the indigenous populations where Santería has taken root.

These prayers will provide a foundation upon which you can build your faith and beliefs. It is through this faith that your prayers will be fulfilled. The devotions within these pages will help you pray consciously, vigorously, sincerely and honestly. True prayer can only come from within yourself.

TOLL FREE: 1 (888) OCCULT - 1

ORIGINAL PUBLICATIONS

- ☐ **HELPING YOURSELF WITH SELECTED PRAYERS;** *Volume 1*; $7.95
- ☐ **HELPING YOURSELF WITH SELECTED PRAYERS:** *Volume 2*; $9.95
- ☐ **ORIGINAL PUBLICATIONS COMPLETE BATH BOOK** - Canizares - $8.95
- ☐ **UNHEXING AND JINX REMOVING;** by Donna Rose - $5.95
- ☐ **SUCCESS AND POWER THROUGH PSALMS;** by Donna Rose - $5.95
- ☐ **MAGICAL RITUALS FOR MONEY;** by Donna Rose - $5.95
- ☐ **DREAM YOUR LUCKY LOTTERY NUMBERS**; Canizares $5.95
- ☐ **PSALM WORKBOOK:** Robert Laremy - $7.95
- ☐ **SPIRITUAL CLEANSINGS & PSYCHIC PROTECTION;** Robert Laremy $8.95
- ☐ **READING YOUR FUTURE IN THE CARDS;** Eden - $6.95
- ☐ **NEW REVISED MASTER BOOK OF CANDLEBURNING;** Gamache - $7.95
- ☐ **THE MAGIC CANDLE;** Charmaine Dey $6.95
- ☐ **NEW REV. 6&7 BKS. OF MOSES;** Wippler $9.95
- ☐ **MYSTERY OF THE LONG LOST 8,9,10TH BOOKS OF MOSES;** Gamache - $7.95
- ☐ **VOODOO & HOODOO**; by Jim Haskins - $16.95
- ☐ **COMPLETE BOOK OF VOODOO:** Robert Pelton $16.95
- ☐ **PAPA JIM'S HERBAL MAGIC WORKBOOK;** Papa Jim - $7.95
- ☐ **HELPING YOURSELF WITH MAGICAL OILS A-Z;** Maria Solomon - $8.95
- ☐ **LOVE CHARMS & SPELLS;** Jade $6.95
- ☐ **MONEY MAGIC;** by Jade - $6.95
- ☐ **PROTECTION CHARMS & SPELLS;** Jade - $5.95
- ☐ **SANTERIA; AFRICAN MAGIC IN LATIN AMERICA;** Wippler $12.95
- ☐ **RITUALS AND SPELLS OF SANTERIA;** Wippler $9.95
- ☐ **MAGICAL HERBAL BATHS OF SANTERIA;** Carlos Montenegro $7.95
- ☐ **POWERS OF THE ORISHAS;** Wippler $9.95
- ☐ **THE BOOK ON PALO;** Raul Canizares $21.95
- ☐ **BRAZILIAN PALO PRIMER:** Robert Laremy $6.95
- ☐ **AGANJU; The Orisha of Volcanoes & Wilderness;** Canizares $5.95
- ☐ **ESHU ELLEGGUA; Orisha of the Crossroad**; Canizares $5.95
- ☐ **SHANGO; Santeria and the Orisha of Thunder**; Canizares $5.95
- ☐ **BABALU AYE; Santeria and the Lord of Pestilence;** Canizares $5.95
- ☐ **OSHUN: Santeria and the Orisha of Love;** Canizares $5.95
- ☐ **OGUN: Santeria and the Warrior Orisha of Iron;** Canizares $5.95
- ☐ **OYA: Santeria and the Orisha of Storms;** Canizares $5.95
- ☐ **YEMAYA: Santeria and the Orisha of the Seven Seas**; Canizares $5.95
- ☐ **ORUNLA: Santeria and the Orisha of Divination**; Canizares $5.95
- ☐ **OSANYIN: Santeria and the Orisha of Lord of Plants**; Canizares $5.95
- ☐ **OBATALA: White Robed King of the Orisha**; Canizares $5.95
- ☐ **AWO: IFA & THE THEOLOGY OF ORISHA DIVINATION;** Fatunmbi $19.95

NAME _____ TELEPHONE _____

ADDRESS _____

CITY _____ STATE _____ ZIP _____

AMERICAN EXPRESS VISA DISCOVER MasterCard   *TOLL FREE* **(888) 622-8581 -OR- (631) 420-4053**

ORIGINAL PUBLICATIONS • P.O. BOX 236, OLD BETHPAGE, NY 11804-0236